Original title:
Tropical Rain, Tropical Sun

Copyright © 2025 Creative Arts Management OÜ
All rights reserved.

Author: Penelope Hawthorne
ISBN HARDBACK: 978-1-80581-492-4
ISBN PAPERBACK: 978-1-80581-019-3
ISBN EBOOK: 978-1-80581-492-4

Dappled Light and Wet Leaves

In the jungle, the shadows play,
A splash of color, bright and gay.
A squirrel slips on a leaf so slick,
And lands with grace, a real comedy trick.

Raindrops dance on the ground below,
Creating puddles for a splashy show.
A frog in a tux jumps with a cheer,
Singing, "Who's the real star around here?"

Flashes of Warmth in the Mist

A parrot squawks in the morning haze,
As sunbeams peek through leafy maze.
The lizard basks with a goofy grin,
Saying, "Five more minutes, let the day begin!"

The heat rolls in, like a neighbor's song,
While ants march by, oh so strong.
One trips and falls, then starts to yell,
"Where's my squad? I'm stuck in this shell!"

A Tapestry of Sincere Showers

The pitter-patter fills the air,
As drips and drops dance everywhere.
A monkey swings, then takes a spill,
Lands in the mud, with a glorious thrill.

A cluster of vines joins the fun,
As droplets keep falling, one by one.
A quick tap dance, slick and spry,
Turns the forest floor into a slippery tie.

Glistening Paths Under Canopies

Beneath the leaves, a snail trots by,
With more than enough to catch the eye.
It glides along, a slow parade,
While butterflies laugh, they've got it made.

The surface shines with a mirror's gleam,
As laughter and joy reign supreme.
A drunken bee buzzes past to see,
"Who knew nature could be this zany?"

The Pulse of Nature's Breath

Woke to splashes, oh what a fate,
The sky's a leaky faucet, one giant crate!
Umbrellas dancing, like they lost their way,
Puddles forming, ready for a play.

The frogs are croaking, singing a tune,
While squirrels slide down a slippery moon.
Raindrops are tickling my nose with glee,
Nature's laughter echoes, just wait and see.

Harmony in Sunlit Puddles

Splash! Jump! And giggle, a forecast of fun,
Reflecting the smiles, under a bright, bold sun.
Each pocket of water, a mirror of cheer,
I see my own face and can't help but leer.

The puddles are planets, on this wacky day,
Where ducks waddle like they're on a ballet.
Jumping from one to the next, what a sight,
In this jig of nature, everything feels right.

Whispers of the Monsoon

Clouds mumble softly, like a secretive friend,
Waiting for lightning to twist and bend.
Without a warning, whoosh! Here it comes,
A drumming on rooftops, creating loud bums.

The animals dash, like they've lost their mind,
Cats in raincoats, oh what a find!
Chickens are flapping, trying to take flight,
Even the grass looks confused in its fright.

Sunlit Lullabies

As bright rays tickle the sleepy old trees,
Birds serenade, singing sweet melodies.
While shadows play hide-and-seek, they tease,
Nature's laughter flows gently with ease.

We dance on the grass, beneath the warm glow,
Chasing the giggles like a fun-loving show.
In each beaming moment, let's wink at the sky,
For every bright giggle makes worries sigh.

The Pulse of Nature's Blessings

Puddles form like tiny pools,
As frogs in hats play jumpy fools.
Umbrellas dance, a funny sight,
While thunder shakes with pure delight.

Coconuts roll like bowling balls,
As laughter bounces off the walls.
Sunbeams peek between the trees,
Tickling leaves in playful tease.

Raindrops wear their silly shoes,
Each splash a joke, no time to snooze.
While rainbows stretch in silly arcs,
Creating color on the parks.

Nature's beat is quite a show,
With giggles swirling, to and fro.
The earth's alive, it winks and spins,
In this grand dance, everyone wins.

Harmony of Shades and Splashes

Splashing puddles, what a scene,
A troop of kids, they laugh and preen.
With water fights and silly grins,
They make the best of all that spins.

Sunshine sneaks, with golden flares,
As birds try on their flashy layers.
Parrots squawk in giddy tunes,
Their colors bright like cartoon moons.

In playful showers, giggles fly,
While flowers dance and butterflies.
Each drop a surprise from the sky,
A playful wink, a cheer, a sigh.

Mirth is found in every gust,
Embracing chaos, joy's a must.
With shades of humor everywhere,
Life's a carnival beyond compare.

Whispers of the Monsoon

Puddles form beneath my shoes,
Frogs leap high with joyful blues.
Umbrella flops and sails away,
Drenched, I laugh—"What a day!"

Clouds are gossiping with the trees,
Raindrops tickle, what a tease.
I dance around with giddy glee,
While soggy squirrels laugh at me.

Sunlit Canopy Dreams

Beneath the beams, a lizard grins,
It wears my lost flip-flop as fins.
The sun's a joker, must be true,
Heating up my picnic stew.

Maracas made of coconuts,
Dance with breezes, shaking butts.
Fruit flies join the wild parade,
While ants march on, unafraid.

Lullabies of Humid Nights

Crickets chirp a serenade,
The air is thick, a warm charade.
Fireflies blink like tiny stars,
As I swat with my candy bars.

The moon's a thief in my backyard,
Stealing snacks, oh, how it's hard!
I giggle at the nighttime freaks,
While wondering if frogs have squeaks.

Golden Drops and Shadowed Leaves

The fruit is dripping, oh so sweet,
With mango juice, I can't compete.
Lemonade smiles in the heat wave,
My drink's a pool, quite the brave.

Branches sway with a cheeky wink,
As I trip on a hidden drink.
Nature's laughs echo in the air,
I'm soaked in joy, without a care.

Colors in the Eye of a Storm

Gray clouds dance with a twist of green,
Yellow ducks join in, a comical scene.
The wind shouts loudly, like a silly mime,
While rain drops giggle, keeping perfect time.

Lightning strikes a pose, what a funny sight,
As thunder laughs, rumbles with delight.
A rainbow pops out, like a cheerful clown,
In this wild circus, no one will frown.

Sweet Aftermath of Showers

Puddles form mirrors, reflecting the skies,
Jumping in joy, like big splashy pies.
The scent of wet earth, oh what a treat,
Flowers wink at us, looking quite neat.

Little frogs croak, like they're in a band,
As ants march along, in a parade so grand.
Sunshine bursts in, like a giggling kid,
With all these shenanigans, nature's a lid!

The Giggle of the Glistening Ground

The ground sparkles bright, as if wearing jewels,
Silly squirrels frolic, acting like fools.
Each raindrop drops jokes, into the mud,
While worms do a dance, creating a thud.

In a puddle deep, splashes cause cheer,
The flowers are laughing, can you hear?
A splash from a foot, brings joy all around,
Oh, the joy of the glistening ground!

Cascades and Rays

Every waterfall tumbles with giggles galore,
As sunlight breaks through, dancing on the floor.
Fish flip and flap, joining the fun,
In this splashy disco under a blazing sun.

Monkeys swing by, throwing coconuts keen,
While parrots squawk jokes that are quite the scene.
With laughter and light, the day's simply grand,
In this carnival world, oh so well planned.

Warmth in the Afternoon Shower

Puddles form like little lakes,
A frog jumps in, it makes me shake.
Umbrellas flip like pirate sails,
While giggling kids tell silly tales.

Raindrops tap a joyful beat,
Splashing shoes, it feels so sweet.
Slippery paths, a dance we try,
As puddles mirror the cloudy sky.

Nature's Brush of Brightness

Sunshine spills like lemonade,
Lemonade stands parade in shade.
A squirrel juggles nuts with flair,
While sunbeams play without a care.

Daisies giggle, swaying wide,
As lizards hop and glide,
The bees wear tiny yellow hats,
And dance around like silly rats.

A Cascade of Radiance

Jellybeans fall from the sky,
Clouds of cotton candy fly.
A rainbow prances, skips around,
While popcorn drizzles to the ground.

A waterfall of giggles sprouts,
Funny faces, joyful shouts.
With every splash, a chuckle grows,
As earth turns into a circus show.

Shimmers of the Ocean Breeze

Waves wave back like playful friends,
Their frothy laughter never ends.
Seagulls strut in silly socks,
As they dive down for what they want.

Breezes dance with twirling grace,
They make the sand jump in place.
A beach ball flies and lands with flair,
While everyone just stops to stare.

Embrace of the Stormy Breeze

The clouds play tag, what a sight,
They dance and swirl, taking flight.
Umbrellas flipped, laughter in the air,
Soggy socks, but who really cares?

A puddle serves as our new pool,
We splash around, feeling like fools.
Lightning strikes, but we're still bold,
With every zap, more stories told.

The Lure of Warmth and Water

Sunshine's here, let's break the norm,
Sunscreen dance, oh how we swarm!
Tanning lotion, oh what a treat,
But greasy burgers can't be beat!

The big waves call, we're on the prowl,
Fishy friends wave with a scowl.
Beachballs bounce, oh what a fight,
We're all just kids in pure delight!

Lush Greens Beneath a Merciless Sky

Greenery waits, oh the sun's not shy,
Plantains giggle as they grow high.
Sweat beads trickle, sliding with flair,
Nature's sauna? We'll take the dare!

The breeze whispers, "Are you still hot?"
I reply, "Just boil me a pot!"
Laughter erupts, it's always a race,
Dashing for shade, a frantic chase!

Cascading Horsepower of Nature

Raindrops drum like a wild machine,
The ground's a stage, for a wet routine.
A muddy slide, we giggle and cheer,
Who knew wet dirt could bring such cheer?

Thunder roars, making fun of our glee,
We hold hands tight, like a splashy spree.
Nature's power, such comic relief,
Drenched with joy, we're the goofball chief!

Shadows in the Downpour

Umbrellas pop up like mushrooms at dawn,
Wink at rubber boots, a watery con.
Puddles become ponds where ducks go to float,
While kids splash around in their grand rubber coat.

Rainy days bring out a dance in the street,
With slips and with slides, it's a muddy retreat.
Laughter will echo, as the sky pours it down,
In a world gone wild, we'll never wear frowns.

Golden Beams and Silver Streams

Sunbeams giggle, dart through the trees,
With shadows that dance in a soft summer breeze.
Dripping icicles from a kid's ice cream cone,
Like a sticky parade, we all share our own.

Lemonade skies with a hint of a splash,
It's a sunshine festival—oh, what a bash!
Sunhats and flip-flops, let fun moments thrive,
With daydreams in colors that come alive.

Dance of the Dewdrops

Dewdrops twirl on the blades of green grass,
A jiggly ballet as breezes all pass.
They giggle and shimmer, a sparkling crew,
In a party of droplets, oh look at them cue!

Caterpillars gossip from leaves in a blur,
While ants join the show, with a wiggle and stir.
Flowers will sway, they could waltz to the tune,
While all of nature hums under the moon.

Radiance After Rainfall

Suds of the sky wash the world with delight,
Colors pop out, everything feels just right.
The sun's cheeky grin wipes the clouds all away,
Now puddles reflect a fairytale play.

Post-storm, the air carries laughter and cheer,
As garden gnomes giggle, no worries near here.
Rain boots on parade, we bounce to the fun,
In the afterglow, it's a whimsical run.

Swaying Palms and Soaked Earth

The palms are doing the hula dance,
While puddles await their wet romance.
Beanies flying off in a breezy play,
Squishy shoes say, 'Let's splash today!'

The clouds are laughing, it's quite a sight,
As surfing squirrels take a quirky flight.
A duck in shades struts on the path,
While rain-soaked socks earn a wet wrath.

Radiance after the Deluge

After the downpour, the sun comes to tease,
While raindrops cling to the tips of the leaves.
A rainbow giggles, stretching so wide,
As flip-flops squeak with a sense of pride.

Lizards sunbathe on warm, steamy stones,
While frogs croak jokes in ridiculous tones.
The earth smells like mischief, fresh and bright,
As puddles reflect winks in the light.

Dancing Shadows in Quiet Valleys

In quiet valleys where shadows prance,
The critters are staging a wild romance.
A caterpillar with moves so slick,
Is stealing the spotlight, doing a flick.

The breeze is giggling, teasing the trees,
While ants make a conga, oh such a tease!
Fireflies twinkle like stars in the day,
As the plants shake it off in a leafy ballet.

Sunbeams Through the Mist

Sunbeams burst through the fog's soft embrace,
Like a toddler in crayons, brightening space.
A peacock struts in his finest display,
While misty cats plot to join the fray.

The air is a circus of scents intertwined,
With coffee and blooms, oh how they aligned!
As laughter erupts from the hills, just so,
In a magical moment where silliness flows.

Drenched in Liquid Gold

A duck in my yard, he wobbles with glee,
Chasing the drops, what a sight to see!
He splashes and dances, his feathers go wild,
While I watch from the porch, feeling like a child.

The trees wear their crowns, all soaked and so bright,
As squirrels slide down like they're on a ride.
Puddles turn into mirrors, reflecting the fun,
While I giggle at nature, all glistening under the sun.

Storms and Hues of Honey

The sky rumbles loud, like a band on a spree,
As I run for my umbrella, what a sight to see!
A rainbow appears, like a smile on a wall,
Reminding us all to just have a ball.

The drops hit the ground, like pop rocks in play,
Each splash brings a giggle, chasing blues away.
And honey-bees buzz with their sweet little tune,
While I dance in the puddles, under the balloon.

The Brightness After the Clouds

The sky clears its throat, and the sun cracks a grin,
As if saying, "Don't worry, the fun can begin!"
Grass sparkles like diamonds, the world feels so new,
I toast with my drink, to the skies that show blue.

A lizard in shades, sunbathing with flair,
While I work on my tan, with nobody a care.
The laughter of kids dances high in the air,
As marigolds bloom, with sunshine to share.

Sun-drenched Moments Between Sprinkles

A parrot caws out, with style and pizzazz,
Holding court on the fence, like he's got a biz.
In between the splashes, we skip and we hop,
While the sun throws confetti, twinkling non-stop.

Flip-flops are flying, and so are the smiles,
Every raindrop a reason to dance for a while.
In shorts and a tank, I twirl at the scene,
With zest that's contagious, I'm living the dream!

The Symphony of Stormy Skies

Puddles on sidewalks dance like clowns,
Umbrellas pop up, like mushrooms in towns.
A tap dance of droplets on tin roofs and trees,
While frogs croak their tunes with the greatest of ease.

Thunder rolls in, it's time to get loud,
Lightning strikes, it's an electrifying crowd.
Birds hide in the branches, peeking out shy,
As laughter erupts from the storm in the sky.

Glimmers Beneath the Canopy

Sunbeams peek through like they're playing hide,
While lizards wear shades, looking cool with pride.
Coconuts giggle, they sway with the breeze,
While monkeys throw parties up high in the trees.

A carnival of colors creates such delight,
Butterflies flutter, a floating stage fight.
Pineapples cheer from their prickly parade,
As smiles bloom bright in nature's grand charade.

Spectrum of the Sky

Daybreak's a painter with hues all around,
Splashes of yellow from sunbeams abound.
Clouds wear their pinks like a fashionable coat,
While seagulls jest, "What a high-flying boat!"

As evening descends, the curtains draw wide,
Stars wink at the moon, glowing with pride.
Fireflies twinkle in a show of their own,
While nature's performers hustle and groan.

Raindrop Serenade

Raindrops tap dance, a merry concert show,
They slip and they slide, what a wild toe-to-toe!
Each splash a giggle, each puddle a song,
As trees sway along, getting groovy and strong.

When sunbeams peek out, they steal the whole scene,
Turning raindrops to gems, oh so bright and serene.
Bugs wear tiny hats, preparing to strut,
In this vibrant play, nobody's a nut!

Afterglow in the Lushness

In the jungle where gorillas play,
The monkeys swing without a delay.
A parrot squawks with a sassy twirl,
While a sloth sleeps like it owns the world.

A toucan struts, its beak on display,
As lizards dance in a club all day.
Coconuts drop, with a thud so loud,
Even the crabs join in, feeling proud.

Murmurs of Leafy Shadows

Underneath the canopy, whispers arise,
Chattering insects in vibrant disguise.
A squirrel plots with nuts on its mind,
While a tortoise grumbles, too slow to find.

There's laughter in puddles, where frogs like to leap,
A dance of delight, they never lose sleep.
The breeze tells secrets, the trees start to sway,
In this leafy theater, it's always play!

Sunlight's Kiss on a Waterfall

Golden beams tickle the waves as they flow,
Fish leap for joy, putting on quite a show.
With splashes and giggles, they swirl all around,
While ducks wear tiny hats, oh what a sound!

The water sparkles, a disco in motion,
As turtles glide by with ultimate devotion.
Sunbathing lizards don shades that are bold,
While otters steal pause for a laugh, uncontrolled.

Raindrops in a Halo

Pitter-patter overhead like a funky tune,
A frog croaks loudly, thinking it's noon.
The ground is a trampoline, bouncy and slick,
While puddles reflect little feet doing tricks.

Worms come out, having the best of the day,
As clouds in their pajamas begin to sway.
Dancing in droplets, they shimmy and glide,
In this playful chaos, none can hide!

Solstice of Serenity

Beneath the sky, a splash of heat,
The sun, a flame, dance on my feet.
Umbrellas pop, a grown-up play,
As we sip drinks, let worries stray.

A gentle breeze, a wild fan,
Blow away troubles, oh yes, we can!
In flip-flops, giggles, twirl around,
Who knew palms could be so profound?

Wet dog shakes, oh what a sight,
Splashing puddles, such pure delight.
We chase our hats as they take flight,
Under giggling clouds, it feels so right.

Dewdrops and Daydreams

Mornings drip with sparkly jewels,
Nature's shower, we dance like fools.
With soggy grass beneath our toes,
We laugh at life as water flows.

A squirt from a hose, a sneaky prank,
Water fights, we're sure to tank.
The lemonade spills, sticky paws,
Sweet summer chaos without a pause.

Sunburned noses, look at us glow,
Not a care for the show we blow.
Running in circles, we're wild and free,
Dewdrops sparkle, oh can't you see?

A Lull in the Leafy Woods

In shady groves where laughter swells,
We tell tall tales and ring like bells.
The birds join in with cheeky glee,
While squirrels judge from a lofty tree.

Picnics spread with crumbs galore,
Ants march in lines, what's in store?
We hide our snacks, then yell and squeak,
As mysteries in the woods we seek.

A tickle from grass brings roars of fun,
Rolling downhill, a race we run.
Chasing shadows, a game we weave,
In leafy retreats, we'll never leave.

Glints of Ya Ya's Glee

Grandma's laughter, what a delight,
Sipping tea in the dappled light.
With crooked glasses and candy stash,
Our secret club, we giggle and clash.

Tropical fruit, a colorful feast,
She dances around like a lively beast.
Slipping on peels, oh what a thrill,
"Too much fun" is our only bill.

The sun's golden rays become our stage,
For silly skits that rampage.
With hugs and kisses, love's the key,
Ya Ya's glee sets our spirits free.

Patters on the Roof

Pitter-patter, the sky's new game,
Tiny dancers play with no shame.
The roof's a stage, a splashy affair,
Even the pots seem to twist and to share.

Raindrops giggle, bouncing along,
The cat's on a mission, singing a song.
Mice in the corner don't know what to do,
While puddles on pavement invite a big shoe!

The gutters are grinning, oh what a show,
Keeping the secrets of where all winds blow.
But in their excitement, they spill all the tea,
So much laughter it feels like a spree!

And when it ends, the sun gives a wink,
A stage covered in sparkles, one can't help but think.
Grab your umbrellas and dance 'round in glee,
Who knew the heavens could be so zany?

The Aroma of Soft Earth

Oh, the smell of damp gives quite the cheer,
A bouquet of mud that's always near.
Nature's perfume after the greet,
A medley of fragrances, oh how sweet!

Worms in tuxedos come out to say hi,
With little top hats, oh me, oh my!
Mushrooms are giggling, looking so bold,
Shouting, "Join us, the story unfolds!"

The flowers trumpeting secrets they've kept,
While under the soil, the critters have slept.
A root's revelry, it's quite a display,
Living it up in their muddy ballet!

And when breezes mingle with scents so divine,
We twirl through the garden, feeling just fine.
Come take a whiff of this earthy delight,
Where nature's aroma makes everything bright!

Glance of the Glorious Day

Oh what a cheer from the morning's first light,
Waking up squirrels with a dance in their flight.
The sun softly tickles the limbs of the trees,
As laughter erupts from the playful sweet breeze.

Chirpy birds gossip, sharing their news,
In feathery suits, they can't help but cruise.
While ants march in rhythm, a miniature band,
Creating a ruckus, oh isn't it grand?

A dog in the grass rolls over with glee,
Chasing thrills like they're setting him free.
The butterflies flutter, with colors so bold,
Stirring up joy with their stories retold!

And when shadows stretch under skies so blue,
Each moment we share feels like something new.
So laugh at the sunshine, let's dance on a whim,
This bustling day gives our lives quite the trim!

Mists and Glimmers of Enchantment

The morning mist weaves a cloak so thin,
Whispering secrets of magic within.
Glimmers of dew, like stars on the grass,
Who knew wet luck could come in a class?

The trees wear their jewels, all shiny and bright,
While squirrels play tag, oh what a sight!
Each leaf is a palette of nature's fine art,
Winking at dreamers who dare to take part.

With giggles of fog, they frolic and prance,
Turning the meadow into a grand dance.
A breeze adds a twist, a playful embrace,
While shadows spin tales of a magical place!

And as the day stretches, the sun finds its way,
Chasing the mischief that lingered to play.
In this world of wonder, where joy spills and sways,
Every glance is a treasure, oh what fun displays!

Serenity Woven in Gold

Laughter dances in the breeze,
Where the palm trees sway with ease.
Banana peels in a playful race,
Slipping smiles on every face.

Coconuts crash like drums so loud,
As we gather, a merry crowd.
With shades so bright, we giggle and play,
Chasing sunbeams all day.

The breeze whispers secrets of bliss,
As mango juice spills from a kiss.
We toast to the clouds, soft and white,
With dreams as sweet as a chocolate bite.

Oh, to be wrapped in this golden glow,
With sunsets that steal the show.
Where laughter meets the evening sky,
And worries flutter gently by.

Gentle Drumming on Canopied Rooftops

Pitter-patter on leafy crowns,
A rhythm that never wears frowns.
The tin roof dances, a jig of glee,
While turtles join in, sipping iced tea.

The monkeys swing, their tunes so bold,
Chasing raindrops like gleaming gold.
And every drip makes a wacky sound,
As puddles form, joy unbound.

A parrot squawks, giving out advice,
On how to stay cool, and play nice.
As laughter rings, and spirits zoom,
Each drop a giggle in the room.

Bamboo chimes play a silly song,
As nature dances all day long.
With every splash, a story's spun,
In this whimsical dance, we're all one.

Where the Horizon Meets Reflection

Palm fronds wave like hands so spry,
As goldfish flip in the shimmering sky.
We chase shadows on sandy shores,
And hunt for treasures in ocean roars.

Waves crash, creating laughter's tune,
As we build castles that touch the moon.
A seagull steals our fries with glee,
The cheeky rascal, oh, what a spree!

Even the jellyfish joins the fun,
With a jig of its own under the sun.
The horizon winks, and time stands still,
As we dance to the ocean's thrill.

In this place where water meets sky,
We find the joy that makes us fly.
With every splash, and every cheer,
Life pours magic into our sphere.

After the Storm: A Sunlit Canvas

Once upon a time, storm clouds laughed,
Dancing with thunder, like a wild craft.
But after the giggles, the sun peeks out,
Where colors whisper, and raindrops shout.

Butterflies burst from their hidden nests,
Wearing rainbows, oh, what a jest!
They flit through beams of golden light,
Creating chuckles in joyful flight.

The world twinkles with droplets' gleam,
Reflecting laughter, like a dream.
With puddles as mirrors, we leap and splash,
Turning the day into a joyous bash.

As the sun giggles and paints the sky,
We spin in circles, letting time fly.
In the aftermath, fun is our king,
As the universe bursts forth, ready to sing.

The Light After the Storm

The clouds had a party, oh what a sight,
Dancing raindrops twirled, under tulip light.
Puddles like mirrors, reflecting the day,
As frogs in tuxedos leaped in dismay.

Then came the sun, wearing sunglasses with flair,
It grinned at the chaos, didn't seem to care.
With a beam of bright laughter, it dried up the shame,
While snails slid along, it played a sly game.

The wind whispered jokes, as it twirled through the trees,
"Did you hear the one 'bout the squawky breeze?"
Everyone chuckled, even the grey clouds,
As soggy old weather turned chatty in crowds.

And the gardens rejoiced, with blooms bright and bold,
They tossed their petal hats, a sight to behold.
Each drop was a tickle, each ray a delight,
For laughter and sunshine danced into the night.

Joyful Currents for the Mind

In the splash of the puddles, a fish took a leap,
Said, "What a wet party! I'm ready for sleep!"
The ducks quacked in chorus, a silly old band,
While the sun shook the droplets from each happy hand.

The laughter of breezes blew soft through the air,
As monkeys played tag, with a whimsy so rare.
Fruit bats with sunglasses formed a jolly crew,
Swinging from branches, singing songs bright and blue.

In the jungle of joy, the colors ran wild,
Every critter a comedian, each plant a sweet child.
Bees buzzed the chorus while ants tapped the beat,
A festival of laughter, oh what a treat!

As dusk dipped in giggles, the moon rose with grace,
With stars joining in for a grand cosmic race.
In the afterglow, a rainbow did curl,
Painting a slippery smile on the world.

Hummingbirds and Hidden Light

In gardens of chuckles, with nectar so sweet,
Hummingbirds zipped by in a flurry of heat.
They sipped on the giggles, then buzzed away fast,
While flowers took selfies, enjoying their blast.

A butterfly flapped, with a wink from its eye,
"Catch me if you can!" it said with a sigh.
The whole scene was silly, yet elegant too,
As colors collided and laughter just flew.

The sun peeked through leaves, playing hide and seek,
While critters called loudly, "Hey, come take a peek!"
They hosted a shindig, made jokes about bugs,
As frogs croaked the punchlines, with squirty love tugs.

In this cheerful tableau, strange friendships were formed,
Each creature took turns, never feeling forlorn.
Joy sparkled one moment, then swayed into night,
With hummingbirds whirling, all twinkling with light.

Rays of Hope Post-Deluge

After the drumming of clouds in a row,
The world wore a grin, with a sunlit bow.
Raindrops like diamonds hung bright from the trees,
As squirrels threw a fiesta, not caring for freeze.

The rabbits wore hats found in yesterday's rain,
They hopped and they twirled, with nary a strain.
A turtle in shades claimed the grassy right field,
While wildflowers giggled, their beauty revealed.

In the midst of the mirth, a parrot exclaimed,
"Dance like there's sunshine, don't be too ashamed!"
So they all formed a conga, a critter parade,
Marching in rhythm, as laughter was made.

With rays shining down, there was joy all around,
Every creature involved, no complaints to be found.
In the mayhem of glee, the sun found its way,
At the end of the storm, joy is here to stay.

Radiant Echoes of an Ancient Earth

A parrot squawks while sipping tea,
An iguana hums a tune with glee.
Palm trees swing in a wild dance,
As crabs form lines and take a chance.

With coconuts as bouncing balls,
The monkeys giggle, then take falls.
Giggling rumors on the breeze,
Dance like shadows beneath the trees.

A sloth takes selfies on a limb,
His smile wide, his pose a whim.
Turtles try to race on sand,
But end up stuck—oh, isn't life grand?

In this land of vivid cheer,
Every critter's voice is clear.
Laughter echoes, day or night,
On ancient earth, what pure delight!

The Kiss of Warmth on Cool Waters

Floating on a leaf, I see
A fish with shades as bright as me.
He wiggles and he starts to sing,
His bubbles round like tiny rings.

A turtle boats on sunny waves,
While otters splash like nimble knaves.
Their joke-telling quite absurd,
For who needs manners; it's just a word!

The frogs host parties on the shore,
With tiny hats; they dance and roar.
They leap and croak in goofy fun,
While sunbeams play and never shun.

Rubber duckies drift past me,
I laugh so hard, I look quite free.
Oh, what bliss upon this sea,
Where warm sun kisses coolness, whee!

Daydreams Amidst Rainy Whispers

Pitter-patter on the leaves,
A message from the wise old thieve.
The raindrops tease, they tap-dance bold,
While snails embrace their shells like gold.

A laughter burst from puddles round,
As frogs in tuxedos leap up and down.
Splashing joy, with added flair,
A slippery show beyond compare.

In each tiny drop, a tale unfolds,
Of mischievous squirrels and moonlit golds.
Raindrops giggle, twirling low,
As umbrellas open like flowers in glow.

Daydreams drift like gentle gusts,
In whispered jokes, we build our trusts.
So, let it rain and let it pour,
For laughter blooms forevermore!

Hues of Joy in Glorious Light

Bright hues stretch across the sky,
As paintbrush clouds drift boldly by.
With laughs that twinkle in the air,
Nature's wonders sparkle everywhere.

Butterflies race with dandelion seeds,
In the silly dance that nature leads.
Each petal winks, a laugh it shares,
A flower girl in sun-kissed flares.

Sunbeams tickle through the leaves,
As lizards strike their best reprieves.
They bask and pose, such trendy sights,
All flaunting joy in dazzling lights.

As dusk draws close, the colors blend,
A symphony that seems to end.
But in the night, the fun won't cease,
With dancing stars, our hearts find peace!

A Palette of Wet and Warm

Puddles in the street, a splashy show,
Rubber ducks afloat, oh what a flow!
Umbrellas dance like fools on a spree,
While flip-flops go diving, just wait and see.

Raindrops waltz on roofs, a merry beat,
Squirrels in galoshes, oh what a treat!
The sun peeks out, a cheeky grin,
And suddenly it's sauna where we begin.

Colors blend as clouds play peek-a-boo,
The world's a canvas, splattered in dew.
Kids in raincoats jump high with glee,
While puddles dare them, "Come splash with me!"

Dancing in the downpour, a slapstick scene,
With laughter bubbling like a fizzy machine.
And when it dries, we're left with a smile,
For every storm's just fun after a while.

Harvest of the Heavens

Banana peels tossed, slip and slide,
As the clouds burst forth, we take it in stride.
A fruit salad sky, lemon and lime,
While squirrels plot mischief, oh what a crime!

Rain or shine, the farm is alive,
Cacti prance while the fruits take a dive.
Melons roll freely, laughing out loud,
As sunshine and showers form a jolly crowd.

Watermelons grow in a puddly contest,
Plump and gleeful, they dance with zest.
Sun-baked tomatoes wearing hats of green,
In this wacky garden, what a scene!

The carrots complain, "We need a tan!"
While beans race the raindrops, "Catch us if you can!"
A harvest of giggles, ripe with cheer,
In this mischief, we all hold dear.

The Pulse of Moist Air

Hummingbirds buzzing with jokes in the breeze,
While raindrops tap dance on soft leafy trees.
The air smells like mischief, sweet with delight,
As fireflies flicker like stars in the night.

Mugs of cocoa in hand, we share what we've found,
While laughter erupts from the sill of each sound.
Pineapples wear shades, feeling quite hip,
While limes roll down hills with a fruity flip.

Bubblegum clouds swirl and twist in the sky,
As giggles pop up, "Oh my, oh my!"
The humidity sweeps with giggles galore,
Turning each corner to open up more.

So let's ride the wind, it's a honking good time,
With jammed-up umbrellas, we'll make the world rhyme.

In this playful pulsation, let's laugh till we're sore,
Underneath the smiling clouds that we adore.

Echoes in the Ebbing Light

Dusk drips with color, a showtime affair,
As giggles echo through the balmy air.
Jellybean sunsets stretch wide and bright,
While the night giggles softly, tucked in tight.

Fireflies gather, a concert of glee,
As frogs croak the rhythm, just you and me.
With headlamps and wishes, we dance round the glow,
In this magic balloon, let your laughter flow.

The wind plays a tune with a whimsical twist,
As shadows chase moonbeams, we can't resist.
The stars wink and shimmer, "What's all the fuss?"
As echoes of fun ride the evening's bus.

So here's to the moments that twinkle and shine,
With whimsies and wishes, our hearts intertwine.
In the fading light, we hold memories tight,
As echoes of laughter dance into the night.

Where Shadows Meet the Light

In the jungle, the sun's a clown,
Playing peek-a-boo in the leafy gown.
Lizards basking on stones, all in a row,
Laughing at the clouds, putting on a show.

Watermelon splashes, oh what a sight,
Chasing raindrops like they're out for a bite.
The squirrels dance in their silly parade,
While the dogs chase their tails, totally afraid.

A rainbow jumps into the fray,
Painting the ground where the monkeys play.
And if you ask the parrot what he's seen,
He'll squawk out stories fit for a queen.

So let the sun and shadows collide,
Creating giggles that cannot hide.
For in this land where laughter is grand,
Every little creature has a game planned.

Sunbeams Dancing on Puddles

With each drop that lands, a splashy bop,
Sunbeams waltz in a mighty hop.
Frogs in tuxedos, oh, what a sight,
Jumping like dancers through morning light.

Squelchy shoes leave a sloppy trail,
As children chase their dreams without fail.
Giggles echo as splashes take flight,
Every puddle's a chance for delight.

A duck in a bow tie quacks out a tune,
While drips from the roof play a jazzy rune.
And if the rain dares to break in a race,
The sun gives a wink, "I'll still win this chase!"

Once the water's all done with the show,
Rainbow confetti dances below.
So let's splash around, in fun we shall bask,
For each little droplet has joy on task.

The Fruitful Overture of the Skies

A fruit salad falls from the clouds above,
Mangoes and bananas, oh how they shove!
The birds wear hats in the fruity feast,
While monkeys munch, to say the least.

Lemons roll down like mischievous balls,
As pineapples giggle, shadowing walls.
The weather is zany, a wild surprise,
With coconuts bouncing, oh what a prize!

Juicy laughter in every bite,
Nature's comedy, such pure delight.
In this quirky garden, fun's on display,
Where every fruit hopes to join the ballet.

So dance to the rhythm of nature's own rhyme,
With sweetness and silliness, oh how sublime!
Let's celebrate laughter in this tasty domain,
For each juicy moment bursts with joy's reign.

Liquid Sunshine

A sip of joy flows from the sky,
Giggling droplets as they fly.
Umbrellas turn into rafts of fun,
Paddling around 'til the day is done.

Clouds like cotton candy drift along,
While rainbows sing a cheerful song.
Drizzles become little toe-tapping tunes,
Dancing all day beneath sun and moons.

Splash parties erupt on the mud-slick ground,
With rubber ducks quacking, merrily found.
Each splash sends giggles into the air,
As puddles form smiles everywhere.

So let's toast to the liquid delight,
And soak in the humor from morning till night.
For every droplet is a chance for cheer,
In this world that sparkles, oh so dear!

Luminous Hues on Rain-Kissed Skin

In puddles deep, they splash and play,
A dance of colors brightening the gray.
Umbrellas flip like fish on a line,
Admiring the polka dots, oh how they shine!

With water guns, they wage a war,
Chasing giggles from door to door.
Rain boots squeak with every bound,
As laughter echoes all around.

The skies drop jewels, a playful tease,
So they scoop and toss with joyful ease.
The world transforms, a lively art,
As showers weave a funny start.

Then sunbeams peek, a cheeky grin,
While dance moves emerge; let the fun begin!
With twirls and spins, embrace the thrill,
In hues of joy, one can't sit still!

The Solace of Soft Drizzles

A gentle tap, a rhythmic tune,
Like whispers shared beneath the moon.
Raindrops tease the sleepy grass,
Sending flowers into a dance class!

Bubbles form on leaf and brook,
In this wet world, take a look!
Slick sidewalks, a slippery slope,
Watch out, my friend, don't lose your hope!

Splash! A leap, a sudden twist,
Tommy's shoes now do the waltz, oh what a list!
While puddles line the way to fun,
"See who's taller!" shouts everyone!

When droplets dwindle, they strike a pose,
As if the sun might steal the show.
A scene so silly, a painted thrill,
In every drizzle, joy does spill!

Verdant Tales Under Blazing Skies

Bright leaves wave at the steamy air,
As critters hold their breath for flair.
A grasshopper croaks a silly song,
While sunbeams blaze, they cheer along!

With lemonade in hand, they lounge and grin,
Drenched in laughter as the fun begins.
Unruly kids in wide-brimmed hats,
Swatting away the sassy brats!

The laughter echoes, a joyful cheer,
As shadows chase away the fear.
In gardens lush, where mischief brews,
A silly parade with no time to lose!

But here comes a cloud, oh what a sight,
Hiding all the sun in a petty fight!
With giggles loud, they promise soon,
Back to the shine — oh what a boon!

Delight in the Coming of Clouds

A fluffy army rolls into town,
The children watch with a curious frown.
Will it rain? Will it pour?
Or merely tease, then leave them wanting more?

As drops descend, their shoes take flight,
Sprinting madly in pure delight.
A slip, a fall, a splashy jump,
Turns into laughter, a cheerful thump!

They gather 'round with cheer to share,
Every trick the raindrops dare.
With teddy bears and clothes to twirl,
In every puddle, they do whirl!

Then sunbeams break — the clouds retreat,
Once more they shine, oh what a feat!
In wet hair and sopping wet socks,
Life's a chuckle, a playful paradox!

The Refreshing Sprinkle

Puddles gleam like disco balls,
Blowing kisses from the falls.
Umbrellas flip like flying fish,
Oh, how I wish for a dry dish!

Meanwhile, frogs host karaoke shows,
Jumping high in rain-soaked clothes.
They croak a tune, it's quite absurd,
As the clouds chuckle, all unheard.

Yet in this battle of wet and wild,
The sun peeks out, a playful child.
With golden rays, it warms the day,
While drizzles dance, then skedaddle away.

A slippery slip and a sudden fall,
Makes for laughter, oh, here we call!
So grab your boots and join the play,
In the splashy world where we all sway!

Mosaic of Light and Water

Bubbles form a sparkling trail,
As rainbows dance, let's set the sail.
A splash of color in the air,
Who needs worries? Let's just care.

Laughing skies and puddles wide,
Playground for a joyful ride.
The sunshine jests, the raindrops cheer,
In this canvas, fun is near.

Little ducks, they waddle forth,
Displaying skills of endless worth.
They take a bath in every shallow,
Making ripples, oh so hallow.

With each drop, a giggle bursts,
A symphony from nature's thirsts.
So grab your hat, let's go outside,
In this mosaic, joy won't hide!

Tides of Warmth and Mist

The air is thick with playful steam,
As laughter bubbles like a dream.
Sweaty brows and shiny backs,
Pet lizards plotting their next tracks.

Misty hugs wrap us so tight,
As the sun smirks, oh what a sight!
The leaves all shimmer, dance, and twirl,
Nature's party, let's give it a whirl!

The floor is slick, be quick on feet,
Watch out for that little comedic heat.
Belly laughs as we slide and glide,
In this sweltering, giggly ride.

So raise a glass of frosty cheer,
To summer's fun, let's hold it dear.
With waves of warmth and waves of jest,
Come join the laughter, it's simply the best!

The Embrace of Blue and Gold

The sky is dressed in a drapery bright,
While raindrops twinkle like stars at night.
On sandy shores where giggles reign,
The sun winks at clouds, what a funny game!

Seashells play hide and seek with feet,
As waves clap hands to a rhythmic beat.
A sandcastle sweet, tilting cute,
Awaits a splash from my muddy boot!

With each wave crash, we burst with glee,
In this concoction of fun, you see.
The breeze brings stories from afar,
As we flip and flop, oh what a czar!

So let the blue and gold unite,
For sunny jokes and rain-drenched delight.
Dive in the laughter, let's all be bold,
In this paradise where joy unfolds!

The Joy of Earthly Kisses

In the midst of the droppin' glee,
A puddle splash, oh, look at me!
Umbrellas dance around like fools,
As rain begins the wettest rules.

Dogs leap high with joyful barks,
Sailing through the water parks!
Puddles become their playful steeds,
Chasing joy among the reeds.

What's that up? A grubby squirrel!
He's dodging drops with quite a twirl!
Nature's circus, wild and bright,
Making fun from day to night.

In the damp, it's clear to see,
Raindrops giggle, wild and free,
With every slip and every splash,
The earthly kisses make a splash!

Bright Drops on Feathery Ferns

Ferns are sweaters, oh so fine,
Draped in beads, they gleam and shine.
Joyful droplets, high and low,
Hugging leaves as they softly glow.

Wiggly worms in lively skirts,
Dance around like happy flirts.
They jiggle past the blushing dew,
In their party, me and you!

Each splash sings a silly tune,
Bouncing up to greet the moon.
A froggy laugh and then a leap,
From those ferns so plush and deep.

The world's a stage, so weird yet grand,
With drops that tickle, chaos unplanned.
Oh, feathery ferns, let's take a chance,
For nature's drops lead us to dance!

The Sparkle of Serendipity

Clouds puff up like cotton candy,
Rain begins—oh, isn't it dandy?
Splashing colors all around,
A joyful symphony is found.

Laughing flowers share a wink,
As drizzles form a liquid blink.
A sneezy bee buzzes with flair,
While petals celebrate the air.

Umbrellas spin like tops in flight,
Comedic sights throughout the night.
Lightning strikes with a cheeky grin,
The universe's giggle begins!

Time slips by in merry jest,
With every droplet, nature's best.
Sparkling joy in every way,
Serendipity leads our play!

Breathe of the Blooming World

Warm breezes tickle blooms awake,
Soft confetti falls, no mistake.
Petals giggle in the sun,
A floral dance has just begun.

Each leaf's a hat for tiny ants,
They march and twirl in silly pants.
Sipping nectar with grand delight,
Their party shifts from day to night.

Butterflies, in costumes bright,
Flutter by in silly flight.
A wobbly dance in fragrant air,
Turning heads, they have their flair.

With every breeze, the laughter swirls,
In this robust and silly world.
Breathe it all, don't let it fade,
In nature's fun, we're all parayed!

www.ingramcontent.com/pod-product-compliance
Lightning Source LLC
Chambersburg PA
CBHW072128070526
44585CB00016B/1573